ABOUT THIS STUDY:

According to the apostle John, true Christ-followers are proven by their love... love that sacrifices as a natural outflow of the regenerated life.

So what does that look like? Scripture paints a pretty clear picture, and it starts with Jesus Himself. His love isn't driven by a self-gratifying emotional outcome. It isn't dependent on the actions of the loved. It cannot be earned. His love is intense, intentional, complete, unfettered and it's active.

True biblical love sacrifices... not for the sake of giving up, but for the sake of giving. It's the heart of Jesus. His love purifies the impure. It heals the broken. It brings living water to the thirsty.

In short, true love does something. Not part way. Not sometimes. Always. That's a tall order. How do you get there? Start with the example and command of Jesus. Lay down your life.

GW00689712

JN 15:12-13

ontrack devotions
EXPEDITION

www.OnTrackDevotions.com

OnTrack Expedition: LaDYL: John 15:12-13

Printed in the United States of America

Any internet addresses, email addresses, phone numbers and physical addresses in this book are accurate at the time of publication. They are
provided as a resource. Pilgrimage Educational Resources does not endorse them or vouch for their content or permanence.

Author: Dwight E. Peterson
Executive Developer: Benjamin J. Wilhite
Graphic design by Lance Young (higherrockcreative.com)

ISBN-13 978-0692254622
ISBN 0692254625

10 9 8 7 6 5 4 3 2 1

PASSAGES (ESV)

John 15:12-13
12 "This is my commandment, that you love one another as I have loved you. 13 Greater love has no one than this, that someone lay down his life for his friends.

Romans 5:6-8
6 For while we were still weak, at the right time Christ died for the ungodly. 7 For one will scarcely die for a righteous person—though perhaps for a good person one would dare even to die— 8 but God shows his love for us in that while we were still sinners, Christ died for us.

John 10:11-15
11 I am the good shepherd. The good shepherd lays down his life for the sheep. 12 He who is a hired hand and not a shepherd, who does not own the sheep, sees the wolf coming and leaves the sheep and flees, and the wolf snatches them and scatters them. 13 He flees because he is a hired hand and cares nothing for the sheep. 14 I am the good shepherd. I know my own and my own know me, 15 just as the Father knows me and I know the Father; and I lay down my life for the sheep.

1 John 3:16-19
16 By this we know love, that he laid down his life for us, and we ought to lay down our lives for the brothers. 17 But if anyone has the world's goods and sees his brother in need, yet closes his heart against him, how does God's love abide in him? 18 Little children, let us not love in word or talk but in deed and in truth. 19 By this we shall know that we are of the truth and reassure our heart before him;

Philippians 2:25-30
25 I have thought it necessary to send to you Epaphroditus my brother and fellow worker and fellow soldier, and your messenger and minister to my need, 26 for he has been longing for you all and has been distressed because you heard that he was ill. 27 Indeed he was ill, near to death. But God had mercy on him, and not only on him but on me also, lest I should have sorrow upon sorrow. 28 I am the more eager to send him, therefore, that you may rejoice at seeing him again, and that I may be less anxious. 29 So receive him in the Lord with all joy, and honor such men, 30 for he nearly died for the work of Christ, risking his life to complete what was lacking in your service to me.

PASSAGE
INTRO NOTES

Record key ideas from the passage introduction or from your first read through the entire passage. Write down any "big questions" on the tag below so you can revisit them during the week.

BIG questions this week...

PRE-EVENT
FRAMING

1: SET GOALS

This exercise is designed to help prepare your heart and mind for the week of your upcoming event. Take some time to get alone and answer them. Good goals should be specific and measurable.

(1) Complete the following sentences to help you formulate some goals for the week:

This week, I hope I...

This week, I hope we as a group...

(2) Complete the following sentences to help you begin to formulate a strategy for seeing the above goals fulfilled:

In light of my answers above, I must...

In light of my answers above, we must...

EXPEDITION

(3) Complete the following sentences to help you formulate a plan to avoid what will derail your goals:

In light of my answers, I must not...

In light of my answers, we must not...

2: PLAN & COMMIT

Take your responses from the previous questions and write out a "personal commitment" for the week. That is, what are you going to personally commit to be doing this week and commit to not be doing. You will sign it and seek out at least one other person on the trip who will read it, pray for its fulfillment, and keep you accountable to it. If possible, seek out a second witness that will not be part of the event group that will pray for you during the event and will check in with you afterward to see how it went.

I, _____, personally commit to

I further commit to not

Name: _____

Signature: _____

Witness#1: _____

Witness#2: _____

Date: ____/____/____

1: JOURNAL

Experiences
What experiences have you faced in the last 24 hours?

Questions
What questions do you find yourself asking?

Conclusions
What kind of conclusions are you coming to about yourself and others?

2: READ JOHN 15:12-13
Read through the passage and record any thoughts or questions which are generated from what you read. In addition, record how this the content of these passages relate to what you are dealing with on the trip.

3: EVALUATE
Answer the questions below based on John 15:12-13.

What is the most loving thing anyone has ever done for you?

What is the most loving thing you have ever done for someone else?

Does love always have to involve sacrifice? Why or Why not?

Are there any circumstances in which this commandment is optional for you? If so, when?

Consider how you lived the last few days... How much does this commandment define the way you've been living?

Are you willing to take a step closer to Jesus? If so, write down one concrete thing you can do today to make a loving sacrifice for someone else. Make it challenging but do-able. Then go do it.

4: INTEGRATE
Spend some time on each of the following activities to get the most out of today's study.

Memorize 1 Jn 3:16-18

Pray
Spend some time praying for yourself and for others in your group.

Commit
In light of what you see in yourself so far, what personal commitment will you make for today? Write it down...

Today, I'm praying for...

I commit to...

2ND DAY
UNLOVEABLE

1: JOURNAL

Experiences
What experiences have you faced in the last 24 hours?

Questions
What questions do you find yourself asking?

Conclusions
What kind of conclusions are you coming to about yourself and others?

EXPEDITION

2: READ ROMANS 5:6-8
Read through the passage and record any thoughts or questions which are generated from what you read. In addition, record how this the content of these passages relate to what you are dealing with on the trip.

3: EVALUATE
Answer the questions below based on Romans 5:6-8

Was there ever a time in your life when you were hard to love? Explain.

Was there anyone who stuck with you through that time even though it was rough? If so, how did that affect you. If not, how did that effect you?

A lot of people think that they have to clean up their sin and failures on their own before God will accept them. What does this passage have to say about that?

How do you tend to respond to people that are hard for you to be around? Are you okay with your answer or do you feel like you need to make some changes?

Spend some time asking God to give you the courage and patience to lay your life down for someone who is tough to be around today.

4: INTEGRATE
Spend some time on each of the following activities to get the most out of today's study.

Memorize 1 Jn 3:16-18
Pray
Spend some time praying for yourself and for others in your group.

Commit
In light of what you see in yourself so far, what personal commitment will you make for today? Write it down...

Today, I'm praying for...

I commit to...

3RD DAY
YOUR ROLE

1: JOURNAL

Experiences
What experiences have you faced in the last 24 hours?

Questions
What questions do you find yourself asking?

Conclusions
What kind of conclusions are you coming to about yourself and others?

2: READ JOHN 10:11-15
Read through the passage and record any thoughts or questions which are generated from what you read. In addition, record how this the content of these passages relate to what you are dealing with on the trip.

3: EVALUATE
Answer the questions below based on John 10:11-15.

Take a good look at the wolf, the hired hand, and the good shepherd. Identify the actions associated with each of them.

What do you think is motivating each of those characters?

If you were one of the sheep, how would you feel about each character? What would you say to each character?

Take a minute and think about the effect you are having on the group this week. Which of the characters you just considered best illustrates your effect on the group?

Identify one thing you can do to better play the role of the Good shepherd for the people you come in contact with today.

4: INTEGRATE
Spend some time on each of the following activities to get the most out of today's study.

Memorize 1 Jn 3:16-18

Pray
Spend some time praying for yourself and for others in your group.

Commit
In light of what you see in yourself so far, what personal commitment will you make for today? Write it down...

Today, I'm praying for...

I commit to...

1: JOURNAL

Experiences
What experiences have you faced in the last 24 hours?

Questions
What questions do you find yourself asking?

Conclusions
What kind of conclusions are you coming to about yourself and others?

2: READ 1 JOHN 3:16-19

Read through the passage and record any thoughts or questions which are generated from what you read. In addition, record how this the content of these passages relate to what you are dealing with on the trip.

3: EVALUATE

Answer the questions below based on 1 John 3:16-19.

If you were to call someone a hypocrite or a poser, what would you mean?

"Actions speak louder than words." Restate that saying in your own words.

Write down some of the good things God has given you. Think in terms of abilities, talents, experiences, relationships, possessions, etc.

Which of those things can you share with people today?

Does the love of God live in you? Prove it.

4: INTEGRATE

Spend some time on each of the following activities to get the most out of today's study.

Memorize 1 Jn 3:16-18

Pray
Spend some time praying for yourself and for others in your group.

Commit
In light of what you see in yourself so far, what personal commitment will you make for today? Write it down...

Today, I'm praying for...

I commit to...

1: JOURNAL

Experiences
What experiences have you faced in the last 24 hours?

Questions
What questions do you find yourself asking?

Conclusions
What kind of conclusions are you coming to about yourself and others?

2: READ PHILIPPIANS 2:25-30

Read through the passage and record any thoughts or questions which are generated from what you read. In addition, record how this the content of these passages relate to what you are dealing with on the trip.

3: EVALUATE
Answer the questions below based on Philippians 2:25-30.

According to this passage, how close were Paul (the writer) and Epaphroditus? What phrases are you basing your answer on?

What do you think Epaphroditus did to become so important to the people around him?

Is there anyone in your life who is like Epaphroditus for you?

People tend to think that the way to become important is to be the smartest, best looking, or most outgoing. According to this passage, what do you think God has to say about that?

What are some steps you need to take to be like Epaphroditus today?

4: INTEGRATE
Spend some time on each of the following activities to get the most out of today's study.

Memorize 1 Jn 3:16-18

Pray
Spend some time praying for yourself and for others in your group.

Commit
In light of what you see in yourself so far, what personal commitment will you make for today? Write it down...

Today, I'm praying for...

I commit to...

1: EVALUATE

This exercise is designed to help discover and record the key takeaways from the week. Take some time to work through the process so you will get the most out of it.

(1) Take some time to read back through the pre trip contract you signed at the beginning of the week.

Write down some of the occasions where you fulfilled your commitment this week.

Write down some of the occasions where you struggled with your commitment this week.

List some of the experiences God used this week to challenge you in light of your commitment.

(2) Read back through your daily journal entries and Bible study notes and answer the questions below.

Are you happy with the way you handled yourself this week in light of all you've learned about laying down your life? Why/Why not?

How do your actions this week compare to the way you live your every-day life back home?

What's the most significant thing you learned about yourself this week?

What's the most significant thing you learned about laying down your life for others?

2: APPLY

This exercise is designed to help connect your key takeaways to "real life" at home. Take some time to work through each of the steps below.

(1) Take a minute and think about what things will be like when you get home. Write down your thoughts.

What are you most looking forward to?

What are you least looking forward to?

(2) Where do you think it'll be most difficult to live out what you've learned?

(3) Where do you think it will be easiest to live out what you've learned?

3: COMMIT

Take your responses from the previous questions and write out a "personal commitment" for your transition to "real life." That is, what are you going to personally commit to be doing and commit to not be doing at home. You will sign it and seek out at least one other person from the trip who will read it, pray for its fulfillment, and keep you accountable to it. Also seek out a key person at home to share your commitment(s) with that will encourage you, pray for you and hold you accountable.

I, _____, personally commit to

I further commit to not

Name: _____

Signature: _____

Witness#1: _____

Witness#2: _____

Date: ____/____/____

MEET THE AUTHOR

Joshua Wilhite grew up in a wilderness ministry environment. He spent 10 summers working with Pilgrimage in a variety of roles and loving every minute of it. After graduating from Baptist Bible College he spent two years working as the Therapeutic Activities Coordinator at a school for troubled youth. He then spent two years working as the outfitting director for Pilgrimage. From there he transitioned to a role as a representative for Baptist Bible College visiting and speaking at over 200 churches and schools. While travelling he earned an MA in Organizational Leadership from Baptist Bible Seminary.

Since 2006 he has been serving as the Pastor of Student Ministries at Solid Rock Bible Church in Plymouth, Michigan. He oversees children's ministry, middle school, high school, and college. Josh is married with three daughters and a little white dog named Brutus (for the girls of course).

Josh has a real passion for authentic growth through discipleship and teaching. He believes that there's nothing more powerful for the teaching of God's word than real life, long-term relationships in a local church. To that end, you'll find him doing his best to help people interact with the Living God one conversation at a time.

Joshua Wilhite

Role: Pastor of Student Ministries

Where: Solid Rock Bible Church (Plymouth, MI)

Family: Married w/3 daughters

Online:

www.SolidRockPlymouth.org

EDITION

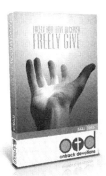

"One of the most effective tools for changing lives I have ever seen... the perfect environment for God to work... resulting in permanent life change."

"Eye opening and life changing."

"...I felt a comeraderie and stretching that met some deeper needs."

"...the most life-changing week of my summer! Thank you so much!"

WILD

WILDERNESS INSTITUTE FOR LEADERSHIP DEVELOPMENT

The GROW System in concentrated format... WILD provides an aggressive multi level learning process. College and Grad credit available. Algonquin Provincial Park - Ontario, Canada

simplyapilgrim.com

Printed in Great Britain
by Amazon